DOVER · THRIFT · EDITIONS

The Concord Hymn and Other Poems

RALPH WALDO EMERSON

DOVER PUBLICATIONS, INC.
New York

DOVER THRIFT EDITIONS

GENERAL EDITOR: STANLEY APPELBAUM
EDITOR OF THIS VOLUME: STEVEN PALMÉ

Bibliographical Note

This Dover edition, first published in 1996, is a new anthology of Ralph Waldo Emerson's poetry selected from *The Early Poems of Ralph Waldo Emerson*, published by T. Y. Crowell & Company, New York, in 1899, and *The Complete Works of Ralph Waldo Emerson* (12 volumes), published by Houghton-Mifflin Co., Boston, in 1903–04.

Library of Congress Cataloging-in-Publication Data

Emerson, Ralph Waldo, 1803–1882.
    The Concord hymn and other poems / Ralph Waldo Emerson.—Dover thrift ed.
        p.   cm.
    Includes index.
    ISBN 0-486-29059-X (pbk.)
    I. Title.
PS1624.C66   1996
811′.3—dc20   95-47925
                                               CIP

Manufactured in the United States of America
Dover Publications, Inc., 31 East 2nd Street, Mineola, N.Y. 11501

Note

RALPH WALDO EMERSON (1803–1882) was a young Unitarian pastor at the Second Church of Boston in 1831, struggling to reconcile his own individualistic views on faith and religion with the rigid formalism of Christian doctrine, when he suffered the loss of his wife, Ellen Tucker. Shortly after Ellen's death he left the Church and traveled through Europe, finally returning to settle in Concord, Massachusetts, in 1833. It was then that, calling upon his skill as an orator so well developed during his time in the pulpit, he began lecturing. His lectures and the collections of essays that followed won him international acclaim as a philosopher, speaker and essayist. He was recognized as one of the first distinctly American voices to emerge during the first half of the nineteenth century. While most often remembered today for his essays and the role they played in forming the philosophy of the Transcendentalists, Emerson viewed himself much differently. "I am a born poet," he wrote in 1835. While publishing only two volumes of verse in his lifetime, he had been writing poetry since his youth and fragments of it appear continuously throughout his journals.

Emerson's approach to poetry was unlike that of his European contemporaries. As in his relationship with the church, he struggled to break out of the rigid, time-honored forms: the fourteen-line stanza of the sonnet, the monotony of heroic couplets and other highly artificial constructions that had characterized "respectable" poetry since the Renaissance. Out of his rebellion emerged a new freedom of style, one of discordant sounds, like those in "Merlin": "The kingly bard / must smite the chords rudely and hard, / As with hammer or with mace." Combined with sometimes awkward rhythms and changing meter, they startled the ear. Each line was shaped to fit an image which, in essence, allowed the content to *dictate* the form instead of being forced to reflect it. Emerson's departure from tradition brought every aspect of language into play in the expression of image, elevating his poetry as a visual and tactile, as well as literary, form.

The content of Emerson's poetry was a fusion of the everyday and what he considered to be universal truths. The calculated, deliberate broadening and narrowing of scope he used so effectively were drawn from his study of, and admiration for, Hindu and Buddhist texts which, he said, dealt "with worlds and pebbles freely." Emerson considered the most ordinary, simple images to be the most powerful and striking in the conveying of great truths. In "The Snow-storm," the common New England occurrence of a winter storm working through the night becomes "astonished Art / To mimic in slow structures, stone by stone / Built in an age, the mad wind's night-work." A list of early Concord landowners that begins "Hamatreya" evolves into a representation of humanity's temporal materialism as seen from the perspective of enduring nature, ending in the song of the Earth, "How am I theirs, / If they cannot hold me, / But I hold them?" In Emerson's hands, the most inauspicious or intimate beginnings consistently lead to the greater ideas embodied in his philosophy, namely mankind's place in the universe.

Emerson's break with poetic tradition was motivated by a deeply personal sense of what poetry, and artistic expression as a whole, was meant to be. He summed up this view in his journals, saying, "When you assume the rhythm of verse and the analogy of Nature, it is making proclamation, 'I am now freed from the trammels of the Apparent; I speak from the Mind.' " This approach to artistic expression was echoed in the free verse of Walt Whitman (who sought Emerson's advice before publishing *Leaves of Grass* [1855]) and Emily Dickinson. The influence of Ralph Waldo Emerson's poetry, through successive generations of writers, can even be seen in the advent of Modernist poetry with T. S. Eliot and Wallace Stevens, who spoke "from the Mind," and broke down the conventions of poetry that Emerson had rebelled against throughout his life.

Contents

MOTTOES FROM THE ESSAYS

The Sphynx

The Sphynx is drowsy,
Her wings are furled,
Her ear is heavy,
She broods on the world. —
"Who'll tell me my secret
The ages have kept?
— I awaited the seer,
While they slumbered and slept; —

The fate of the manchild,
The meaning of man;
Known fruit of the unknown,
Dædalian plan;
Out of sleeping a waking,
Out of waking a sleep,
Life death overtaking,
Deep underneath deep.

Erect as a sunbeam
Upspringeth the palm;
The elephant browses
Undaunted and calm;
In beautiful motion
The thrush plies his wings;
Kind leaves of his covert!
Your silence he sings.

The waves unashamed
In difference sweet,
Play glad with the breezes,
Old playfellows meet.
The journeying atoms,
Primordial wholes,
Firmly draw, firmly drive,
By their animate poles.

Sea, earth, air, sound, silence,
Plant, quadruped, bird,
By one music enchanted,
One deity stirred,

1

Each the other adorning,
Accompany still;
Night veileth the morning,
The vapor the hill.

The babe by its mother
Lies bathed in joy,
Glide its hours uncounted,
The sun is its toy;
Shines the peace of all being
Without cloud in its eyes,
And the sum of the world
In soft miniature lies.

But man crouches and blushes,
Absconds and conceals,
He creepeth and peepeth,
He palters and steals;
Infirm, melancholy,
Jealous glancing around,
An oaf, an accomplice,
He poisons the ground.

Out spoke the great mother
Beholding his fear,
At the sound of her accents
Cold shuddered the sphere; —
Who has drugged my boy's cup,
Who has mixed my boy's bread?
Who with sadness and madness
Has turned the manchild's head?" —

I heard a poet answer
Aloud and cheerfully,
"Say on, sweet Sphynx! thy dirges
Are pleasant songs to me.
Deep love lieth under
These pictures of time,
They fade in the light of
Their meaning sublime.

The fiend that man harries,
Is love of the Best;
Yawns the Pit of the Dragon

Lit by rays from the Blest.
The Lethe of Nature
Can't trance him again,
Whose soul sees the Perfect,
Which his eyes seek in vain.

Profounder, profounder,
Man's spirit must dive;
To his aye-rolling orbit
No goal will arrive.
The heavens that draw him
With sweetness untold,
Once found, — for new heavens
He spurneth the old.

Pride ruined the angels,
Their shame them restores,
And the joy that is sweetest
Lurks in stings of remorse.
Have I a lover
Who is noble and free, —
I would he were nobler
Than to love me.

Eterne alternation
Now follows, now flies,
And under pain, pleasure,
Under pleasure, pain lies.
Love works at the centre,
Heart-heaving alway;
Forth speed the strong pulses
To the borders of day.

Dull Sphynx, Jove keep thy five wits!
Thy sight is growing blear,
Rue, myrrh, and cummin for the Sphynx,
Her muddy eyes to clear."
The old Sphynx bit her thick lip, —
"Who taught thee me to name?
I am thy spirit, yoke-fellow!
Of thine eye I am eyebeam.

Thou art the unanswered question;
Couldst see thy proper eye,

Alway it asketh, asketh,
And each answer is a lie.
So take thy quest through nature,
It through thousand natures ply,
Ask on, thou clothed eternity, —
Time is the false reply."

Uprose the merry Sphynx,
And crouched no more in stone,
She melted into purple cloud,
She silvered in the moon,
She spired into a yellow flame,
She flowered in blossoms red,
She flowed into a foaming wave,
She stood Monadnoc's head.[1]

Through a thousand voices
Spoke the universal dame,
"Who telleth one of my meanings,
Is master of all I am."

Each and All

Little thinks, in the field, yon red-cloaked clown,
Of thee, from the hill-top looking down;
And the heifer, that lows in the upland farm,
Far-heard, lows not thine ear to charm;
The sexton[2] tolling the bell at noon,
Dreams not that great Napoleon
Stops his horse, and lists with delight,
Whilst his files sweep round yon Alpine height;
Nor knowest thou what argument
Thy life to thy neighbor's creed has lent:
All are needed by each one,
Nothing is fair or good alone.

---

[1] A mountain of resistant rock rising from an eroded plain. From *Mt. Monadnock*, New Hampshire.

[2] Gravedigger.

I thought the sparrow's note from heaven,
Singing at dawn on the alder bough;
I brought him home in his nest at even; —
He sings the song, but it pleases not now;
For I did not bring home the river and sky;
He sang to my ear; they sang to my eye.

The delicate shells lay on the shore;
The bubbles of the latest wave
Fresh pearls to their enamel gave;
And the bellowing of the savage sea
Greeted their safe escape to me;
I wiped away the weeds and foam,
And fetched my sea-born treasures home;
But the poor, unsightly, noisome things
Had left their beauty on the shore
With the sun, and the sand, and the wild uproar.

The lover watched his graceful maid
As 'mid the virgin train she strayed,
Nor knew her beauty's best attire
Was woven still by the snow-white quire;
At last she came to his hermitage,
Like the bird from the woodlands to the cage, —
The gay enchantment was undone,
A gentle wife, but fairy none.

Then I said, "I covet Truth;
Beauty is unripe childhood's cheat, —
I leave it behind with the games of youth."
As I spoke, beneath my feet
The ground-pine curled its pretty wreath,
Running over the club-moss burrs;
I inhaled the violet's breath;
Around me stood the oaks and firs;
Pine cones and acorns lay on the ground;
Above me soared the eternal sky,
Full of light and deity;
Again I saw, again I heard,
The rolling river, the morning bird; —
Beauty through my senses stole,
I yielded myself to the perfect whole.

The Problem

I like a church, I like a cowl,
I love a prophet of the soul,
And on my heart monastic aisles
Fall like sweet strains or pensive smiles;
Yet not for all his faith can see,
Would I that cowled churchman be.
Why should the vest on him allure,
Which I could not on me endure?

Not from a vain or shallow thought
His awful Jove young Phidias[1] brought;
Never from lips of cunning fell
The thrilling Delphic oracle;
Out from the heart of nature rolled
The burdens of the Bible old;
The litanies of nations came,
Like the volcano's tongue of flame,
Up from the burning core below,
The canticles of love and woe.
The hand that rounded Peter's dome,[2]
And groined the aisles of Christian Rome,
Wrought in a sad sincerity,
Himself from God he could not free;
He builded better than he knew,
The conscious stone to beauty grew.

Know'st thou what wove yon woodbird's nest
Of leaves and feathers from her breast;
Or how the fish outbuilt its shell,
Painting with morn each annual cell;
Or how the sacred pine tree adds
To her old leaves new myriads?
Such and so grew these holy piles,
Whilst love and terror laid the tiles.
Earth proudly wears the Parthenon

---

[1] A Greek sculptor (5th century B.C.).

[2] Michelangelo Buonarroti (1475–1564), the Italian artist who also painted the ceiling of the Sistine Chapel.

As the best gem upon her zone;
And Morning opes with haste her lids
To gaze upon the Pyramids;
O'er England's abbeys bends the sky
As on its friends with kindred eye;
For out of Thought's interior sphere
These wonders rose to upper air,
And nature gladly gave them place,
Adopted them into her race,
And granted them an equal date
With Andes and with Ararat.

These temples grew as grows the grass,
Art might obey but not surpass.
The passive Master lent his hand
To the vast soul that o'er him planned,
And the same power that reared the shrine,
Bestrode the tribes that knelt within.
Even the fiery Pentecost
Girds with one flame the Countless host,
Trances the heart through chanting quires,
And through the priest the mind inspires.

The word unto the prophet spoken
Was writ on tables yet unbroken;
The word by seers or sibyls told
In groves of oak, or fanes of gold,
Still floats upon the morning wind,
Still whispers to the willing mind.
One accent of the Holy Ghost
The heedless world hath never lost.

I know what say the Fathers wise,
The Book itself before me lies,
Old *Chrysostom*,[1] best Augustine,
And he who blent both in his line,
The younger *Golden-lips* or mines,
Taylor, the Shakspeare of divines,
His words are music in my ear,

---

[1] St. John Chrysostom (4th century A.D.), one of the early archbishops of Constantinople, renowned for his eloquence.

I see his cowled portrait dear,
And yet for all his faith could see,
I would not the good bishop be.

Uriel[1]

It fell in the ancient periods
Which the brooding soul surveys,
Or ever the wild Time coined itself
Into calendar months and days.

This was the lapse of Uriel,
Which in Paradise befell.
Once among the Pleiads[2] walking,
SAID[3] overheard the young gods talking,
And the treason too long pent
To his ears was evident.
The young deities discussed
Laws of form and metre just,
Orb, quintessence, and sunbeams,
What subsisteth, and what seems.
One, with low tones that decide,
And doubt and reverend use defied,
With a look that solved the sphere,
And stirred the devils everywhere,
Gave his sentiment divine
Against the being of a line:
"Line in nature is not found,
Unit and universe are round;
In vain produced, all rays return,
Evil will bless, and ice will burn."
As Uriel spoke with piercing eye,
A shudder ran around the sky;
The stern old war-gods shook their heads;
The seraphs frowned from myrtle-beds;
Seemed to the holy festival,
The rash word boded ill to all;

---

[1] One of the archangels of Christian legend and the angel of the sun in Milton's *Paradise Lost* (Bk. III, ll. 648–57).

[2] The seven nymphs of Diana, Roman goddess of the hunt and a symbol of chastity.

[3] Mosharref od-Din ibn Mosleh od-Din Sa'adi, a Persian poet (1213–1292).

The balance-beam of Fate was bent;
The bonds of good and ill were rent;
Strong Hades could not keep his own,
But all slid to confusion.

A sad self-knowledge withering fell
On the beauty of Uriel.
In heaven once eminent, the god
Withdrew that hour into his cloud,
Whether doomed to long gyration
In the sea of generation,
Or by knowledge grown too bright
To hit the nerve of feebler sight.
Straightway a forgetting wind
Stole over the celestial kind,
And their lips the secret kept,
If in ashes the fibre-seed slept.
But now and then truth-speaking things
Shamed the angels' veiling wings,
And, shrilling from the solar course,
Or from fruit of chemic force,
Procession of a soul in matter,
Or the speeding change of water,
Or out of the good of evil born,
Came Uriel's voice of cherub scorn,
And a blush tinged the upper sky,
And the gods shook, they knew not why.

Mithridates[1]

I cannot spare water or wine,
Tobacco-leaf, or poppy, or rose;
From the earth-poles to the Line,
All between that works or grows,
Every thing is kin of mine.

Give me agates for my meat,
Give me cantharids[2] to eat,

---

[1] The king of Pontus in the 1st century B.C. who developed an immunity to poison by taking small doses daily (from Pliny's *Natural History*).

[2] A preparation of dried blister-beetles once used as an aphrodisiac (Spanish Fly).

From air and ocean bring me foods,
From all zones and altitudes.

From all natures, sharp and slimy,
Salt and basalt, wild and tame,
Tree, and lichen, ape, sea-lion,
Bird and reptile be my game.

Ivy for my fillet band,
Blinding dogwood[3] in my hand,
Hemlock for my sherbet cull me,
And the prussic juice[4] to lull me,
Swing me in the upas boughs,[5]
Vampire-fanned, when I carouse.

Too long shut in strait and few,
Thinly dieted on dew,
I will use the world, and sift it,
To a thousand humors shift it,
As you spin a cherry.
O doleful ghosts, and goblins merry,
O all you virtues, methods, mights;
Means, appliances, delights;
Reputed wrongs, and braggart rights;
Smug routine, and things allowed;
Minorities, things under cloud!
Hither! take me, use me, fill me,
Vein and artery, though ye kill me;
God! I will not be an owl,
But sun me in the Capitol.

---

[3] Poison sumac.

[4] Prussic acid, a form of cyanide.

[5] A tree found in tropical Asia, the sap of which is used for poison darts.

Hamatreya[1]

Minott, Lee, Willard, Hosmer, Meriam, Flint,
Possessed the land, which rendered to their toil
Hay, corn, roots, hemp, flax, apples, wool, and wood.
Each of these landlords walked amidst his farm,
Saying, " 'Tis mine, my children's, and my name's.
How sweet the west wind sounds in my own trees;
How graceful climb those shadows on my hill;
I fancy those pure waters and the flags
Know me as does my dog: we sympathize,
And, I affirm, my actions smack of the soil."
Where are those men? Asleep beneath their grounds,
And strangers, fond as they, their furrows plough.
Earth laughs in flowers to see her boastful boys
Earth proud, proud of the earth which is not theirs;
Who steer the plough, but cannot steer their feet
Clear of the grave.—
They added ridge to valley, brook to pond,
And sighed for all that bounded their domain,
"This suits me for a pasture; that's my park,
We must have clay, lime, gravel, granite-ledge,
And misty lowland where to go for peat.
The land is well,—lies fairly to the south.
'Tis good, when you have crossed the sea and back,
To find the sitfast acres where you left them."
Ah! the hot owner sees not Death, who adds
Him to his land, a lump of mould the more.
Hear what the Earth says:

EARTH-SONG

Mine and yours,
Mine not yours.
Earth endures,
Stars abide,

---

[1] A variation of "Maitreya," from the sacred Hindu text *Vishnu Purana*. Maitreya is the bodhisattva who is to appear as a Buddha 5000 years after the death of Gautama, the historical Buddha.

Shine down in the old sea,
Old are the shores,
But where are old men?
I who have seen much,
Such have I never seen.
The lawyer's deed
Ran sure
In tail
To them and to their heirs
Who shall succeed
Without fail
For evermore.

Here is the land,
Shaggy with wood,
With its old valley,
Mound, and flood. —
But the heritors —
Fled like the flood's foam;
The lawyer, and the laws,
And the kingdom,
Clean swept herefrom.

They called me theirs,
Who so controlled me;
Yet every one
Wished to stay, and is gone.
How am I theirs,
If they cannot hold me,
But I hold them?

When I heard the Earth-song,
I was no longer brave;
My avarice cooled
Like lust in the chill of the grave.

Good-by

Good-by, proud world, I'm going home,
Thou'rt not my friend, and I'm not thine;
Long through thy weary crowds I roam;

A river-ark on the ocean brine,
Long I've been tossed like the driven foam,
But now, proud world, I'm going home.

Good-by to Flattery's fawning face,
To Grandeur, with his wise grimace,
To upstart Wealth's averted eye,
To supple Office low and high,
To crowded halls, to court, and street,
To frozen hearts, and hasting feet,
To those who go, and those who come,
Good-by, proud world, I'm going home.

I'm going to my own hearth-stone
Bosomed in yon green hills, alone,
A secret nook in a pleasant land,
Whose groves the frolic fairies planned;
Where arches green the livelong day
Echo the blackbird's roundelay,
And vulgar feet have never trod
A spot that is sacred to thought and God.

Oh, when I am safe in my sylvan home,
I tread on the pride of Greece and Rome;
And when I am stretched beneath the pines
Where the evening star so holy shines,
I laugh at the lore and the pride of man,
At the sophist schools, and the learned clan;
For what are they all in their high conceit,
When man in the bush with God may meet.

The Rhodora:[1]

ON BEING ASKED, WHENCE IS THE FLOWER?

In May, when sea-winds pierced our solitudes,
I found the fresh Rhodora in the woods,
Spreading its leafless blooms in a damp nook,
To please the desert and the sluggish brook.
The purple petals fallen in the pool

---

[1] A variety of flowering shrub found in Canada and New England.

Made the black water with their beauty gay;
Here might the red-bird come his plumes to cool,
And court the flower that cheapens his array.
Rhodora! if the sages ask thee why
This charm is wasted on the earth and sky,
Tell them, dear, that, if eyes were made for seeing,
Then beauty is its own excuse for being;
Why thou wert there, O rival of the rose!
I never thought to ask; I never knew;
But in my simple ignorance suppose
The self-same power that brought me there, brought you.

The Humblebee

Burly dozing humblebee!
Where thou art is clime for me.
Let them sail for Porto Rique,
Far-off heats through seas to seek,
I will follow thee alone,
Thou animated torrid zone!
Zig-zag steerer, desert-cheerer,
Let me chase thy waving lines,
Keep me nearer, me thy hearer,
Singing over shrubs and vines.

Insect lover of the sun,
Joy of thy dominion!
Sailor of the atmosphere,
Swimmer through the waves of air,
Voyager of light and noon,
Epicurean of June,
Wait I prithee, till I come
Within ear-shot of thy hum, —
All without is martyrdom.

When the south wind, in May days,
With a net of shining haze,
Silvers the horizon wall,
And, with softness touching all,
Tints the human countenance

With a color of romance,
And, infusing subtle heats,
Turns the sod to violets,
Thou in sunny solitudes,
Rover of the underwoods,
The green silence dost displace,
With thy mellow breezy bass.

Hot midsummer's petted crone,
Sweet to me thy drowsy tune,
Telling of countless sunny hours,
Long days, and solid banks of flowers,
Of gulfs of sweetness without bound
In Indian wildernesses found,
Of Syrian peace, immortal leisure,
Firmest cheer and bird-like pleasure.

Aught unsavory or unclean,
Hath my insect never seen,
But violets and bilberry bells,
Maple sap and daffodels,
Grass with green flag half-mast high,
Succory to match the sky,
Columbine with horn of honey,
Scented fern, and agrimony,
Clover, catchfly, adders-tongue,
And brier-roses dwelt among;
All beside was unknown waste,
All was picture as he passed.

Wiser far than human seer,
Yellow-breeched philosopher!
Seeing only what is fair,
Sipping only what is sweet,
Thou dost mock at fate and care,
Leave the chaff and take the wheat.
When the fierce north-western blast
Cools sea and land so far and fast,
Thou already slumberest deep, —
Woe and want thou canst out-sleep, —
Want and woe which torture us,
Thy sleep makes ridiculous.

Berrying

"May be true what I had heard,
Earth's a howling wilderness
Truculent with fraud and force,"
Said I, strolling through the pastures,
And along the riverside.
Caught among the blackberry vines,
Feeding on the Ethiops sweet,
Pleasant fancies overtook me:
I said, "What influence me preferred
Elect to dreams thus beautiful?"
The vines replied, "And didst thou deem
No wisdom to our berries went?"

The Snow-storm

Announced by all the trumpets of the sky
Arrives the snow, and, driving o'er the fields,
Seems nowhere to alight: the whited air
Hides hills and woods, the river and the heaven,
And veils the farm-house at the garden's end.
The steed and traveller stopped, the courier's feet
Delayed, all friends shut out, the housemates sit
Around the radiant fireplace, enclosed
In a tumultuous privacy of storm.
     Come, see the north wind's masonry.
Out of an unseen quarry evermore
Furnished with tile, the fierce artificer
Curves his white bastions with projected roof
Round every windward stake, or tree, or door.
Speeding, the myriad-handed, his wild work
So fanciful, so savage, naught cares he
For number or proportion.   Mockingly
On coop or kennel he hangs Parian wreaths;
A swan-like form invests the hidden thorn;
Fills up the farmer's lane from wall to wall,
Maugre the farmer's sighs, and at the gate

A tapering turret overtops the work.
And when his hours are numbered, and the world
Is all his own, retiring, as he were not,
Leaves, when the sun appears, astonished Art
To mimic in slow structures, stone by stone
Built in an age, the mad wind's night-work,
The frolic architecture of the snow.

Fable

The mountain and the squirrel
Had a quarrel,
And the former called the latter, "little prig":
Bun replied,
You are doubtless very big,
But all sorts of things and weather
Must be taken in together
To make up a year,
And a sphere.
And I think it no disgrace
To occupy my place.
If I'm not so large as you,
You are not so small as I,
And not half so spry:
I'll not deny you make
A very pretty squirrel track;
Talents differ; all is well and wisely put;
If I cannot carry forests on my back,
Neither can you crack a nut.

Ode

INSCRIBED TO WILLIAM H. CHANNING[1]

Though loth to grieve
The evil time's sole patriot,

---

[1] William H. Channing (1810–1880) was a clergyman and abolitionist who urged Emerson to become more outspoken about his antislavery position.

I cannot leave
My buried thought
For the priest's cant,
Or statesman's rant.

If I refuse
My study for their politique,
Which at the best is trick,
The angry muse
Puts confusion in my brain.

But who is he that prates
Of the culture of mankind,
Of better arts and life?
Go, blind worm, go,
Behold the famous States
Harrying Mexico
With rifle and with knife.

Or who, with accent bolder,
Dare praise the freedom-loving mountaineer?
I found by thee, O rushing Contoocook!
And in thy valleys, Agiochook!
The jackals of the negro-holder.

The God who made New Hampshire
Taunted the lofty land
With little men.
Small bat and wren
House in the oak.
If earth fire cleave
The upheaved land, and bury the folk,
The southern crocodile would grieve.

Virtue palters, right is hence,
Freedom praised but hid;
Funeral eloquence
Rattles the coffin-lid.

What boots thy zeal,
O glowing friend,
That would indignant rend
The northland from the south?
Wherefore? To what good end?

Boston Bay and Bunker Hill
Would serve things still:
Things are of the snake.

The horseman serves the horse,
The neat-herd serves the neat,
The merchant serves the purse,
The eater serves his meat;
'Tis the day of the chattel,
Web to weave, and corn to grind,
Things are in the saddle,
And ride mankind.

There are two laws discrete
Not reconciled,
Law for man, and law for thing;
The last builds town and fleet,
But it runs wild,
And doth the man unking.

'Tis fit the forest fall,
The steep be graded,
The mountain tunnelled,
The land shaded,
The orchard planted,
The globe tilled,
The prairie planted,
The steamer built.

Let man serve law for man,
Live for friendship, live for love,
For truth's and harmony's behoof;
The state may follow how it can,
As Olympus follows Jove.
Yet do not I implore
The wrinkled shopman to my sounding woods,
Nor bid the unwilling senator
Ask votes of thrushes in the solitudes.
Every one to his chosen work.
Foolish hands may mix and mar,
Wise and sure the issues are.
Round they roll, till dark is light,
Sex to sex, and even to odd;

The over-God,
Who marries Right to Might,
Who peoples, unpeoples,
He who exterminates
Races by stronger races,
Black by white faces,
Knows to bring honey
Out of the lion,
Grafts gentlest scion
On Pirate and Turk.

The Cossack eats Poland,[2]
Like stolen fruit;
Her last noble is ruined,
Her last poet mute;
Straight into double band
The victors divide,
Half for freedom strike and stand,
The astonished muse finds thousands at her side.

Astræa[1]

Himself it was who wrote
His rank, and quartered his own coat.
There is no king nor sovereign state
That can fix a hero's rate;
Each to all is venerable,
Cap-a-pie invulnerable,
Until he write, where all eyes rest,
Slave or master on his breast.

I saw men go up and down
In the country and the town,
With this prayer upon their neck,
"Judgment and a judge we seek."
Not to monarchs they repair,
Nor to learned jurist's chair,

---

[2] Refers to the Russian Repression of the 1830 Polish Nationalist uprising.

[1] Greek goddess of Justice.

But they hurry to their peers,
To their kinsfolk and their dears,
Louder than with speech they pray,
What am I? companion; say.

And the friend not hesitates
To assign just place and mates,
Answers not in word or letter,
Yet is understood the better; —
Is to his friend a looking-glass,
Reflects his figure that doth pass.
Every wayfarer he meets
What himself declared, repeats;
What himself confessed, records;
Sentences him in his words,
The form is his own corporal form,
And his thought the penal worm.

Yet shine for ever virgin minds,
Loved by stars and purest winds,
Which, o'er passion throned sedate,
Have not hazarded their state,
Disconcert the searching spy,
Rendering to a curious eye
The durance of a granite ledge
To those who gaze from the sea's edge.
It is there for benefit,
It is there for purging light,
There for purifying storms,
And its depths reflect all forms;
It cannot parley with the mean,
Pure by impure is not seen.
For there's no sequestered grot,
Lone mountain tarn, or isle forgot,
But justice journeying in the sphere
Daily stoops to harbor there.

Etienne de la Boéce[1]

I serve you not, if you I follow,
Shadow-like, o'er hill and hollow,
And bend my fancy to your leading,
All too nimble for my treading.
When the pilgrimage is done,
And we've the landscape overrun,
I am bitter, vacant, thwarted,
And your heart is unsupported.
Vainly valiant, you have missed
The manhood that should yours resist,
Its complement; but if I could
In severe or cordial mood
Lead you rightly to my altar,
Where the wisest muses falter,
And worship that world-warning spark
Which dazzles me in midnight dark,
Equalizing small and large,
While the soul it doth surcharge,
That the poor is wealthy grown,
And the hermit never alone,
The traveller and the road seem one
With the errand to be done; —
That were a man's and lover's part,
That were Freedom's whitest chart.

"Suum Cuique"[2]

The rain has spoiled the farmer's day;
Shall sorrow put my books away?
Thereby are two days lost:

---

[1] Etienne de la Boétie (1530–1563) was a poet and the friend of the French philosopher Michel de Montaigne. His early death inspired Montaigne to write his famous *Essais* (1580) on facing death and suffering.

[2] Latin: "To each his own."

Nature shall mind her own affairs,
I will attend my proper cares,
In rain, or sun, or frost.

Compensation

Why should I keep holiday,
When other men have none?
Why but because when these are gay,
I sit and mourn alone.

And why when mirth unseals all tongues
Should mine alone be dumb?
Ah! late I spoke to silent throngs,
And now their hour is come.

Forbearance

Hast thou named all the birds without a gun;
Loved the wood-rose, and left it on its stalk;
At rich men's tables eaten bread and pulse;
Unarmed, faced danger with a heart of trust;
And loved so well a high behavior
In man or maid, that thou from speech refrained,
Nobility more nobly to repay? —
O be my friend, and teach me to be thine!

Give All to Love

Give all to love;
Obey thy heart;
Friends, kindred, days,
Estate, good fame,
Plans, credit, and the muse;
Nothing refuse.

'Tis a brave master,
Let it have scope,
Follow it utterly,

Hope beyond hope;
High and more high,
It dives into noon,
With wing unspent,
Untold intent;
But 'tis a god,
Knows its own path,
And the outlets of the sky.

'Tis not for the mean,
It requireth courage stout,
Souls above doubt,
Valor unbending;
Such 'twill reward,
They shall return
More than they were,
And ever ascending.

Leave all for love; —
Yet, hear me, yet,
One word more thy heart behoved,
One pulse more of firm endeavor,
Keep thee to-day,
To-morrow, for ever,
Free as an Arab
Of thy beloved.
Cling with life to the maid;
But when the surprise,
Vague shadow of surmise,
Flits across her bosom young
Of a joy apart from thee,
Free be she, fancy-free,
Do not thou detain a hem,
Nor the palest rose she flung
From her summer diadem.

Though thou loved her as thyself,
As a self of purer clay,
Tho' her parting dims the day,
Stealing grace from all alive,
Heartily know,
When half-gods go,
The gods arrive.

Merlin[1]

I

Thy trivial harp will never please
Or fill my craving ear;
Its chords should ring as blows the breeze
Free, peremptory, clear.
No jingling serenader's art,
Nor tinkle of piano strings,
Can make the wild blood start
In its mystic springs.
The kingly bard
Must smite the chords rudely and hard,
As with hammer or with mace,
That they may render back
Artful thunder that conveys
Secrets of the solar track,
Sparks of the supersolar blaze.
Merlin's blows are strokes of fate,
Chiming with the forest-tone,
When boughs buffet boughs in the wood;
Chiming with the gasp and moan
Of the ice-imprisoned flood;
With the pulse of manly hearts,
With the voice of orators,
With the din of city arts,
With the cannonade of wars,
With the marches of the brave,
And prayers of might from martyrs' cave.

Great is the art,
Great be the manners of the bard!
He shall not his brain encumber
With the coil of rhythm and number,
But, leaving rule and pale forethought,
He shall aye climb
For his rhyme:
Pass in, pass in, the angels say,

---

[1] Refers to a legendary 6th-century Welsh poet.

In to the upper doors;
Nor count compartments of the floors,
But mount to Paradise
By the stairway of surprise.

Blameless master of the games,
King of sport that never shames;
He shall daily joy dispense
Hid in song's sweet influence.
Things more cheerly live and go,
What time the subtle mind
Plays aloud the tune whereto
Their pulses beat,
And march their feet,
And their members are combined.

By Sybarites[2] beguiled
He shall no task decline;
Merlin's mighty line,
Extremes of nature reconciled,
Bereaved a tyrant of his will,
And made the lion mild.
Songs can the tempest still,
Scattered on the stormy air,
Mould the year to fair increase,
And bring in poetic peace.

He shall not seek to weave,
In weak unhappy times,
Efficacious rhymes;
Wait his returning strength.
Bird, that from the nadir's floor,
To the zenith's top could soar,
The soaring orbit of the muse exceeds that journey's length!

Nor, profane, affect to hit
Or compass that by meddling wit,
Which only the propitious mind
Publishes when 'tis inclined.
There are open hours
When the god's will sallies free,

---

[2] Inhabitants of Sybaris, a Greek city infamous for its wealth and decadence, destroyed in 510 B.C.

And the dull idiot might see
The flowing fortunes of a thousand years;
Sudden, at unawares,
Self-moved fly-to the doors,
Nor sword of angels could reveal
What they conceal.

II

The rhyme of the poet
Modulates the king's affairs,
Balance-loving nature
Made all things in pairs.
To every foot its antipode,
Each color with its counter glowed,
To every tone beat answering tones,
Higher or graver;
Flavor gladly blends with flavor;
Leaf answers leaf upon the bough,
And match the paired cotyledons.
Hands to hands, and feet to feet,
In one body grooms and brides;
Eldest rite, two married sides
In every mortal meet.
Light's far furnace shines,
Smelting balls and bars,
Forging double stars,
Glittering twins and trines.
The animals are sick with love,
Lovesick with rhyme;
Each with all propitious Time
Into chorus wove.

Like the dancers' ordered band,
Thoughts come also hand in hand,
In equal couples mated,
Or else alternated,
Adding by their mutual gage
One to other health and age.
Solitary fancies go
Short-lived wandering to and fro,
Most like to bachelors,
Or an ungiven maid,

Not ancestors,
With no posterity to make the lie afraid,
Or keep truth undecayed.

Perfect paired as eagle's wings,
Justice is the rhyme of things;
Trade and counting use
The self-same tuneful muse;
And Nemesis,
Who with even matches odd,
Who athwart space redresses
The partial wrong,
Fills the just period,
And finishes the song.

Subtle rhymes with ruin rife
Murmur in the house of life,
Sung by the Sisters[3] as they spin;
In perfect time and measure, they
Build and unbuild our echoing clay,
As the two twilights of the day
Fold us music-drunken in.

Bacchus[1]

Bring me wine, but wine which never grew
In the belly of the grape,
Or grew on vine whose taproots reaching through
Under the Andes to the Cape,
Suffered no savor of the world to 'scape.
Let its grapes the morn salute
From a nocturnal root
Which feels the acrid juice
Of Styx and Erebus,
And turns the woe of night,
By its own craft, to a more rich delight.

---

[3] Clotho, Lachesis and Atropos, the Fates of Greek myth who spun, twisted and cut the Thread of Life.

[1] Roman God of wine and revelry.

We buy ashes for bread,
We buy diluted wine;
Give me of the true,
Whose ample leaves and tendrils curled
Among the silver hills of heaven,
Draw everlasting dew;
Wine of wine,
Blood of the world,
Form of forms and mould of statures,
That I, intoxicated,
And by the draught assimilated,
May float at pleasure through all natures,
The bird-language rightly spell,
And that which roses say so well.

Wine that is shed
Like the torrents of the sun
Up the horizon walls;
Or like the Atlantic streams which run
When the South Sea calls.

Water and bread;
Food which needs no transmuting,
Rainbow-flowering, wisdom-fruiting;
Wine which is already man,
Food which teach and reason can.

Wine which music is;
Music and wine are one;
That I, drinking this,
Shall hear far chaos talk with me,
Kings unborn shall walk with me,
And the poor grass shall plot and plan
What it will do when it is man:
Quickened so, will I unlock
Every crypt of every rock.

I thank the joyful juice
For all I know;
Winds of remembering
Of the ancient being blow,
And seeming-solid walls of use
Open and flow.

Pour, Bacchus, the remembering wine;
Retrieve the loss of me and mine;
Vine for vine be antidote,
And the grape requite the lote.
Haste to cure the old despair,
Reason in nature's lotus drenched,
The memory of ages quenched; —
Give them again to shine.
Let wine repair what this undid,
And where the infection slid,
And dazzling memory revive.

Refresh the faded tints,
Recut the aged prints,
And write my old adventures, with the pen
Which, on the first day, drew
Upon the tablets blue
The dancing Pleiads, and the eternal men.

Merops[1]

What care I, so they stand the same, —
Things of the heavenly mind, —
How long the power to give them fame
Tarries yet behind?

Thus far to-day your favors reach,
O fair, appeasing Presences!
Ye taught my lips a single speech,
And a thousand silences.

Space grants beyond his fated road
No inch to the god of day,
And copious language still bestowed
One word, no more, to say.

---

[1] A soothsayer in Homer's *Iliad*. The name is derived from the Greek "meropos" which means "speaking articulately."

Holidays

From fall to spring the russet acorn,
Fruit beloved of maid and boy,
Lent itself beneath the forest
To be the children's toy.

Pluck it now; in vain: thou canst not,
Its root has pierced yon shady mound,
Toy no longer, it has duties;
It is anchored in the ground.

Year by year the rose-lipped maiden,
Play-fellow of young and old,
Was frolic sunshine, dear to all men,
More dear to one than mines of gold.

Whither went the lovely hoyden?[1] —
Disappeared in blessed wife,
Servant to a wooden cradle,
Living in a baby's life.

Still thou playest; — short vacation
Fate grants each to stand aside;
Now must thou be man and artist;
'Tis the turning of the tide.

Xenophanes[2]

By fate, not option, frugal nature gave
One scent to hyson and to wallflower,
One sound to pine-groves and to water-falls,
One aspect to the desert and the lake,
It was her stern necessity. All things
Are of one pattern made; bird, beast, and plant,

---

[1] Carefree girl.

[2] Greek philosopher (ca. 570–480 B.C.) who argued for "cosmic" monotheism, i.e., the universe itself as God.

Song, picture, form, space, thought, and character,
Deceive us, seeming to be many things,
And are but one. Beheld far off, they part
As God and Devil; bring them to the mind,
They dull its edge with their monotony.
To know the old element explore a new,
And in the second reappears the first.
The specious panorama of a year
But multiplies the image of a day,
A belt of mirrors round a taper's flame,
And universal nature through her vast
And crowded whole, an infinite paroquet,
Repeats one cricket note.

The Day's Ration

When I was born,
From all the seas of strength Fate filled a chalice,
Saying, This be thy portion, child; this chalice,
Less than a lily's, thou shalt daily draw
From my great arteries; nor less, nor more.
All substances the cunning chemist Time
Melts down into that liquor of my life,
Friends, foes, joys, fortunes, beauty, and disgust,
And whether I am angry or content,
Indebted or insulted, loved or hurt,
All he distils into sidereal wine,
And brims my little cup; heedless, alas!
Of all he sheds how little it will hold,
How much runs over on the desert sands.
If a new muse draw me with splendid ray,
And I uplift myself into her heaven,
The needs of the first sight absorb my blood,
And all the following hours of the day
Drag a ridiculous age.
To-day, when friends approach, and every hour
Brings book or starbright scroll of genius
The tiny cup will hold not a bead more,
And all the costly liquor runs to waste,
Nor gives the jealous time one diamond drop
So to be husbanded for poorer days.
Why need I volumes, if one word suffice?

Why need I galleries, when a pupil's draught
After the master's sketch, fills and o'erfills
My apprehension? Why should I roam,
Who cannot circumnavigate the sea
Of thoughts and things at home, but still adjourn
The nearest matters to another moon?
Why see new men
Who have not understood the old?

Dirge

Knows he who tills this lonely field
To reap its scanty corn,
What mystic fruit his acres yield
At midnight and at morn?

In the long sunny afternoon,
The plain was full of ghosts,
I wandered up, I wandered down,
Beset by pensive hosts.

The winding Concord gleamed below,
Pouring as wide a flood
As when my brothers long ago,
Came with me to the wood.

But they are gone, — the holy ones,
Who trod with me this lonely vale,
The strong, star-bright companions
Are silent, low, and pale.

My good, my noble, in their prime,
Who made this world the feast it was,
Who learned with me the lore of time,
Who loved this dwelling-place.

They took this valley for their toy,
They played with it in every mood,
A cell for prayer, a hall for joy,
They treated nature as they would.

They colored the horizon round,
Stars flamed and faded as they bade,
All echoes hearkened for their sound,
They made the woodlands glad or mad.

I touch this flower of silken leaf
Which once our childhood knew,
Its soft leaves wound me with a grief
Whose balsam never grew.

Hearken to yon pine warbler
Singing aloft in the tree;
Hearest thou, O traveller!
What he singeth to me?

Not unless God made sharp thine ear
With sorrow such as mine,
Out of that delicate lay couldst thou
The heavy dirge divine.

Go, lonely man, it saith,
They loved thee from their birth,
Their hands were pure, and pure their faith,
There are no such hearts on earth.

Ye drew one mother's milk,
One chamber held ye all;
A very tender history
Did in your childhood fall.

Ye cannot unlock your heart,
The key is gone with them;
The silent organ loudest chants
The master's requiem.

Threnody[1]

The south-wind brings
Life, sunshine, and desire,
And on every mount and meadow
Breathes aromatic fire,
But over the dead he has no power,
The lost, the lost he cannot restore,

---

[1] An elegy. Emerson wrote this poem for his son Waldo ("the wondrous child"), who died in 1842 at the age of five.

And, looking over the hills, I mourn
The darling who shall not return.

I see my empty house,
I see my trees repair their boughs,
And he, — the wondrous child,
Whose silver warble wild
Outvalued every pulsing sound
Within the air's cerulean round,
The hyacinthine boy, for whom
Morn well might break, and April bloom,
The gracious boy, who did adorn
The world whereinto he was born,
And by his countenance repay
The favor of the loving Day,
Has disappeared from the Day's eye;
Far and wide she cannot find him,
My hopes pursue, they cannot bind him.
Returned this day the south-wind searches
And finds young pines and budding birches,
But finds not the budding man;
Nature who lost him, cannot remake him;
Fate let him fall, Fate can't retake him;
Nature, Fate, men, him seek in vain.

And whither now, my truant wise and sweet,
Oh, whither tend thy feet?
I had the right, few days ago,
Thy steps to watch, thy place to know;
How have I forfeited the right?
Hast thou forgot me in a new delight?
I hearken for thy household cheer,
O eloquent child!
Whose voice, an equal messenger,
Conveyed thy meaning mild.
What though the pains and joys
Whereof it spoke were toys
Fitting his age and ken; —
Yet fairest dames and bearded men,
Who heard the sweet request
So gentle, wise, and grave,
Bended with joy to his behest,

And let the world's affairs go by,
Awhile to share his cordial game,
Or mend his wicker wagon frame,
Still plotting how their hungry ear
That winsome voice again might hear,
For his lips could well pronounce
Words that were persuasions.

Gentlest guardians marked serene
His early hope, his liberal mien,
Took counsel from his guiding eyes
To make this wisdom earthly wise.
Ah! vainly do these eyes recall
The school-march, each day's festival,
When every morn my bosom glowed
To watch the convoy on the road; —
The babe in willow wagon closed,
With rolling eyes and face composed,
With children forward and behind,
Like Cupids studiously inclined,
And he, the Chieftain, paced beside,
The centre of the troop allied,
With sunny face of sweet repose,
To guard the babe from fancied foes.
The little Captain innocent
Took the eye with him as he went,
Each village senior paused to scan
And speak the lovely caravan.

From the window I look out
To mark thy beautiful parade
Stately marching in cap and coat
To some tune by fairies played;
A music heard by thee alone
To works as noble led thee on.
Now love and pride, alas, in vain,
Up and down their glances strain.
The painted sled stands where it stood,
The kennel by the corded wood,
The gathered sticks to stanch the wall
Of the snow-tower, when snow should fall,
The ominous hole he dug in the sand,
And childhood's castles built or planned.

His daily haunts I well discern,
The poultry yard, the shed, the barn,
And every inch of garden ground
Paced by the blessed feet around,
From the road-side to the brook,
Whereinto he loved to look.
Step the meek birds where erst they ranged,
The wintry garden lies unchanged,
The brook into the stream runs on,
But the deep-eyed Boy is gone.

On that shaded day,
Dark with more clouds than tempests are,
When thou didst yield thy innocent breath
In bird-like heavings unto death,
Night came, and Nature had not thee, —
I said, we are mates in misery.
The morrow dawned with needless glow,
Each snow-bird chirped, each fowl must crow,
Each tramper started, — but the feet
Of the most beautiful and sweet
Of human youth had left the hill
And garden, — they were bound and still,
There's not a sparrow or a wren,
There's not a blade of autumn grain,
Which the four seasons do not tend,
And tides of life and increase lend,
And every chick of every bird,
And weed and rock-moss is preferred.
O ostriches' forgetfulness!
O loss of larger in the less!
Was there no star that could be sent,
No watcher in the firmament,
No angel from the countless host,
That loiters round the crystal coast,
Could stoop to heal that only child,
Nature's sweet marvel undefiled,
And keep the blossom of the earth,
Which all her harvests were not worth?
Not mine, I never called thee mine,
But nature's heir, — if I repine,
And, seeing rashly torn and moved,
Not what I made, but what I loved.

Grow early old with grief that then
Must to the wastes of nature go, —
'Tis because a general hope
Was quenched, and all must doubt and grope.
For flattering planets seemed to say,
This child should ills of ages stay, —
By wondrous tongue and guided pen
Bring the flown muses back to men. —
Perchance, not he, but nature ailed,
The world, and not the infant failed,
It was not ripe yet, to sustain
A genius of so fine a strain,
Who gazed upon the sun and moon
As if he came unto his own,
And pregnant with his grander thought,
Brought the old order into doubt.
Awhile his beauty their beauty tried,
They could not feed him, and he died,
And wandered backward as in scorn
To wait an Æon to be born.
Ill day which made this beauty waste;
Plight broken, this high face defaced!
Some went and came about the dead,
And some in books of solace read,
Some to their friends the tidings say,
Some went to write, some went to pray,
One tarried here, there hurried one,
But their heart abode with none.
Covetous death bereaved us all
To aggrandize one funeral.
The eager Fate which carried thee
Took the largest part of me.
For this losing is true dying,
This is lordly man's down-lying,
This is slow but sure reclining,
Star by star his world resigning.

    O child of Paradise!
Boy who made dear his father's home
In whose deep eyes
Men read the welfare of the times to come;
I am too much bereft;
The world dishonored thou hast left;

O truths and natures costly lie;
O trusted, broken prophecy!
O richest fortune sourly crossed;
Born for the future, to the future lost!

The deep Heart answered, Weepest thou?
Worthier cause for passion wild,
If I had not taken the child.
And deemest thou as those who pore
With aged eyes short way before?
Think'st Beauty vanished from the coast
Of matter, and thy darling lost?
Taught he not thee, — the man of eld,
Whose eyes within his eyes beheld
Heaven's numerous hierarchy span
The mystic gulf from God to man?
To be alone wilt thou begin,
When worlds of lovers hem thee in?
To-morrow, when the masks shall fall
That dizen nature's carnival,
The pure shall see, by their own will,
Which overflowing love shall fill, —
'Tis not within the force of Fate
The fate-conjoined to separate.
But thou, my votary, weepest thou?
I gave thee sight, where is it now?
I taught thy heart beyond the reach
Of ritual, Bible, or of speech;
Wrote in thy mind's transparent table
As far as the incommunicable;
Taught thee each private sign to raise
Lit by the supersolar blaze.
Past utterance and past belief,
And past the blasphemy of grief,
The mysteries of nature's heart, —
And though no muse can these impart,
Throb thine with nature's throbbing breast,
And all is clear from east to west.

I came to thee as to a friend,
Dearest, to thee I did not send
Tutors, but a joyful eye,
Innocence that matched the sky,
Lovely locks a form of wonder,

Laughter rich as woodland thunder;
That thou might'st entertain apart
The richest flowering of all art;
And, as the great all-loving Day
Through smallest chambers takes its way,
That thou might'st break thy daily bread
With Prophet, Saviour, and head;
That thou might'st cherish for thine own
The riches of sweet Mary's Son,
Boy-Rabbi, Israel's Paragon:
And thoughtest thou such guest
Would in thy hall take up his rest?
Would rushing life forget its laws,
Fate's glowing revolution pause?
High omens ask diviner guess,
Not to be conned to tediousness.
And know, my higher gifts unbind
The zone that girds the incarnate mind,
When the scanty shores are full
With Thought's perilous whirling pool,
When frail Nature can no more, —
Then the spirit strikes the hour,
My servant Death with solving rite
Pours finite into infinite.
Wilt thou freeze love's tidal flow,
Whose streams through nature circling go?
Nail the star struggling to its track
On the half-climbed Zodiack?
Light is light which radiates,
Blood is blood which circulates,
Life is life which generates,
And many-seeming life is one, —
Wilt thou transfix and make it none,
Its onward stream too starkly pent
In figure, bone, and lineament?

Wilt thou uncalled interrogate
Talker! the unreplying fate?
Nor see the Genius of the whole
Ascendant in the private soul,
Beckon it when to go and come,
Self-announced its hour of doom.
Fair the soul's recess and shrine,

Magic-built, to last a season,
Masterpiece of love benign!
Fairer than expansive reason
Whose omen 'tis, and sign.
Wilt thou not ope this heart to know
What rainbows teach and sunsets show,
Verdict which accumulates
From lengthened scroll of human fates,
Voice of earth to earth returned,
Prayers of heart that inly burned;
Saying, *what is excellent,*
As God lives, is permanent,
Hearts are dust, hearts' loves remain,
Heart's love will meet thee again.
Revere the Maker; fetch thine eye
Up to His style, and manners of the sky.
Not of adamant and gold
Built He heaven stark and cold,
No, but a nest of bending reeds,
Flowering grass and scented weeds,
Or like a traveller's fleeting tent,
Or bow above the tempest pent,
Built of tears and sacred flames,
And virtue reaching to its aims;
Built of furtherance and pursuing,
Not of spent deeds, but of doing.
Silent rushes the swift Lord
Through ruined systems still restored,
Broad-sowing, bleak and void to bless,
Plants with worlds the wilderness,
Waters with tears of ancient sorrow
Apples of Eden ripe to-morrow;
House and tenant go to ground,
Lost in God, in Godhead found.

Concord Hymn

SUNG AT THE COMPLETION OF CONCORD MONUMENT,
    APRIL 19, 1836

By the rude bridge that arched the flood,
Their flag to April's breeze unfurled,

Here once the embattled farmers stood,
And fired the shot heard round the world.

The foe long since in silence slept,
Alike the Conqueror silent sleeps,
And Time the ruined bridge has swept
Down the dark stream which seaward creeps.

On this green bank, by this soft stream,
We set to-day a votive stone,
That memory may their deed redeem,
When like our sires our sons are gone.

Spirit! who made those freemen dare
To die, or leave their children free,
Bid time and nature gently spare
The shaft we raise to them and Thee.

Brahma[1]

If the red slayer think he slays,
    Or if the slain think he is slain,[2]
They know not well the subtle ways
    I keep, and pass, and turn again.

Far or forgot to me is near;
    Shadow and sunlight are the same;
The vanished gods to me appear;
    And one to me are shame and fame.

They reckon ill who leave me out;
    When me they fly, I am the wings;
I am the doubter and the doubt,
    And I the hymn the Brahmin sings.

The strong gods pine for my abode,
    And pine in vain the sacred Seven;
But thou, meek lover of the good!
    Find me, and turn thy back on heaven.

---

[1] The priestly caste of the Hindu religion.

[2] "If . . . slain": from *Bhagavadgita* 2:62–64: "He who shall say, 'Lo! I have slain a man!' / He who shall think, 'Lo! I am slain!' those both / Know naught! Life cannot slay. Life is not slain!"

Voluntaries

I

Low and mournful be the strain,
Haughty thought be far from me;
Tones of penitence and pain,
Moanings of the tropic sea;
Low and tender in the cell
Where a captive sits in chains,
Crooning ditties treasured well
From his Afric's torrid plains.
Sole estate his sire bequeathed, —
Hapless sire to hapless son, —
Was the wailing song he breathed,
And his chain when life was done.

What his fault, or what his crime?
Or what ill planet crossed his prime?
Heart too soft and will too weak
To front the fate that crouches near, —
Dove beneath the vulture's beak; —
Will song dissuade the thirsty spear?
Dragged from his mother's arms and breast,
Displaced, disfurnished here,
His wistful toil to do his best
Chilled by a ribald jeer.
Great men in the Senate sate,
Sage and hero, side by side,
Building for their sons the State,
Which they shall rule with pride.
They forbore to break the chain
Which bound the dusky tribe,
Checked by the owners' fierce disdain,
Lured by 'Union' as the bribe.
Destiny sat by, and said,
'Pang for pang your seed shall pay,
Hide in false peace your coward head,
I bring round the harvest day.'

II

Freedom all winged expands,
Nor perches in a narrow place;
Her broad van seeks unplanted lands;
She loves a poor and virtuous race.
Clinging to a colder zone
Whose dark sky sheds the snowflake down,
The snowflake is her banner's star,
Her stripes the boreal streamers are.
Long she loved the Northman well;
Now the iron age is done,
She will not refuse to dwell
With the offspring of the Sun;
Foundling of the desert far,
Where palms plume, siroccos blaze,
He roves unhurt the burning ways
In climates of the summer star.
He has avenues to God
Hid from men of Northern brain,
Far beholding, without cloud,
What these with slowest steps attain.
If once the generous chief arrive
To lead him willing to be led,
For freedom he will strike and strive,
And drain his heart till he be dead.

III

In an age of fops and toys,
Wanting wisdom, void of right,
Who shall nerve heroic boys
To hazard all in Freedom's fight, —
Break sharply off their jolly games,
Forsake their comrades gay
And quit proud homes and youthful dames
For famine, toil and fray?
Yet on the nimble air benign
Speed nimbler messages,
That waft the breath of grace divine
To hearts in sloth and ease.
So nigh is grandeur to our dust,
So near is God to man,

When Duty whispers low, *Thou must*,
The youth replies, *I can*.

IV

O, well for the fortunate soul
Which Music's wings infold,
Stealing away the memory
Of sorrows new and old!
Yet happier he whose inward sight,
Stayed on his subtile thought,
Shuts his sense on toys of time,
To vacant bosoms brought.
But best befriended of the God
He who, in evil times,
Warned by an inward voice,
Heeds not the darkness and the dread,
Biding by his rule and choice,
Feeling only the fiery thread
Leading over heroic ground,
Walled with mortal terror round,
To the aim which him allures,
And the sweet heaven his deed secures.
Peril around, all else appalling,
Cannon in front and leaden rain
Him duty through the clarion calling
To the van called not in vain.

    Stainless soldier on the walls,
Knowing this, — and knows no more, —
Whoever fights, whoever falls,
Justice conquers evermore,
Justice after as before, —
And he who battles on her side,
God, though he were ten times slain,
Crowns him victor glorified,
Victor over death and pain.

V

Blooms the laurel which belongs
To the valiant chief who fights;
I see the wreath, I hear the songs
Lauding the Eternal Rights,

Victors over daily wrongs:
Awful victors, they misguide
Whom they will destroy,
And their coming triumph hide
In our downfall, or our joy:
They reach no term, they never sleep,
In equal strength through space abide;
Though, feigning dwarfs, they crouch and creep,
The strong they slay, the swift outstride:
Fate's grass grows rank in valley clods,
And rankly on the castled steep, —
Speak it firmly, these are gods,
All are ghosts beside.

Days

Daughters of Time, the hypocritic Days,
Muffled and dumb like barefoot dervishes,
And marching single in an endless file,
Bring diadems and fagots in their hands.
To each they offer gifts after his will,
Bread, kingdoms, stars, and sky that holds them all.
I, in my pleached garden, watched the pomp,
Forgot my morning wishes, hastily
Took a few herbs and apples, and the Day
Turned and departed silent. I, too late,
Under her solemn fillet saw the scorn.

Waldeinsamkeit[1]

I do not count the hours I spend
In wandering by the sea;
The forest is my loyal friend,
Like God it useth me.

In plains that room for shadows make
Of skirting hills to lie,
Bound in by streams which give and take
Their colors from the sky;

---

[1] German: Forest Solitude.

Or on the mountain-crest sublime,
Or down the oaken glade,
O what have I to do with time?
For this the day was made.

Cities of mortals woe-begone
Fantastic care derides,
But in the serious landscape lone
Stern benefit abides.

Sheen will tarnish, honey cloy,
And merry is only a mask of sad,
But, sober on a fund of joy,
The woods at heart are glad.

There the great Planter plants
Of fruitful worlds the grain,
And with a million spells enchants
The souls that walk in pain.

Still on the seeds of all he made
The rose of beauty burns;
Through times that wear and forms that fade,
Immortal youth returns.

The black ducks mounting from the lake,
The pigeon in the pines,
The bittern's boom, a desert make
Which no false art refines.

Down in yon watery nook,
Where bearded mists divide,
The gray old gods whom Chaos knew,
The sires of Nature, hide.

Aloft, in secret veins of air,
Blows the sweet breath of song,
O, few to scale those uplands dare,
Though they to all belong!

See thou bring not to field or stone
The fancies found in books;
Leave authors' eyes, and fetch your own,
To brave the landscape's looks.

Oblivion here thy wisdom is,
Thy thrift, the sleep of cares;

For a proud idleness like this
Crowns all thy mean affairs.

Freedom

Once I wished I might rehearse
Freedom's pæan in my verse,
That the slave who caught the strain
Should throb until he snapped his chain.
But the Spirit said, 'Not so;
Speak it not, or speak it low;
Name not lightly to be said,
Gift too precious to be prayed,
Passion not to be expressed
But by heaving of the breast:
Yet, — wouldst thou the mountain find
Where this deity is shrined,
Who gives to seas and sunset skies
Their unspent beauty of surprise,
And, when it lists him, waken can
Brute or savage into man;
Or, if in thy heart he shine,
Blends the starry fates with thine,
Draws angels nigh to dwell with thee,
And makes thy thoughts archangels be;
Freedom's secret wilt thou know? —
Counsel not with flesh and blood;
Loiter not for cloak or food;
Right thou feelest, rush to do.'

The Apology

Think me not unkind and rude
   That I walk alone in grove and glen;
I go to the god of the wood
   To fetch his word to men.

Tax not my sloth that I
   Fold my arms beside the brook;
Each cloud that floated in the sky
   Writes a letter in my book.

Chide me not, laborious band,
    For the idle flowers I brought;
Every aster in my hand
    Goes home loaded with a thought.

There was never mystery
    But 'tis figured in the flowers;
Was never secret history
    But birds tell it in the bowers.

One harvest from thy field
    Homeward brought the oxen strong;
A second crop thine acres yield,
    Which I gather in a song.

Maia[1]

Illusion works impenetrable,
Weaving webs innumerable,
Her gay pictures never fail,
Crowds each on other, veil on veil,
Charmer who will be believed
By man who thirsts to be deceived.

Illusions like the tints of pearl,
Or changing colors of the sky,
Or ribbons of a dancing girl
That mend her beauty to the eye.

The cold gray down upon the quinces lieth
And the poor spinners weave their webs thereon
To share the sunshine that so spicy is.

Samson stark, at Dagon's[2] knee,
Gropes for columns strong as he;
When his ringlets grew and curled,
Groped for axle of the world.

But Nature whistled with all her winds,
Did as she pleased and went her way.

---

[1] Hindu: "Illusion."

[2] Dagon was the god of the Philistines whose temple Samson destroyed (Judges 16:23–31).

MOTTOES FROM THE ESSAYS

Self-Reliance

Henceforth, please God, forever I forego
The yoke of men's opinions. I will be
Light-hearted as a bird, and live with God.
I find him in the bottom of my heart,
I hear continually his voice therein.

. . . .

The little needle always knows the North,
The little bird remembereth his note,
And this wise Seer within me never errs.
I never taught it what it teaches me;
I only follow, when I act aright.

Friendship

A ruddy drop of manly blood
The surging sea outweighs,
The world uncertain comes and goes,
The lover rooted stays.
I fancied he was fled,
And, after many a year,
Glowed unexhausted kindliness
Like daily sunrise there.
My careful heart was free again, —
O friend, my bosom said,
Through thee alone the sky is arched,
Through thee the rose is red,
All things through thee take nobler form,
And look beyond the earth,
And is the mill-round of our fate
A sun-path in thy worth.
Me too thy nobleness has taught
To master my despair;
The fountains of my hidden life
Are through thy friendship fair.

Experience

The lords of life, the lords of life, —
I saw them pass
In their own guise,
Like and unlike,
Portly and grim, —
Use and Surprise,
Surface and Dream,
Succession swift and spectral Wrong,
Temperament without a tongue,
And the inventor of the game
Omnipresent without name; —
Some to see, some to be guessed,
They marched from east to west:
Little man, least of all,
Among the legs of his guardians tall,
Walked about with puzzled look.
Him by the hand dear Nature took,
Dearest Nature, strong and kind,
Whispered, 'Darling, never mind!
To-morrow they will wear another face,
The founder thou; these are thy race!'

Fate

Deep in the man sits fast his fate
To mould his fortunes, mean or great:
Unknown to Cromwell as to me
Was Cromwell's measure or degree;
Unknown to him as to his horse,
If he than his groom be better or worse.
He works, plots, fights, in rude affairs,
With squires, lords, kings, his craft compares,
Till late he learned, through doubt and fear,
Broad England harbored not his peer:
Obeying time, the last to own
The Genius from its cloudy throne.
For the prevision is allied

Unto the thing so signified;
Or say, the foresight that awaits
Is the same Genius that creates.

Nature[1]

I

A subtle chain of countless rings
The next unto the farthest brings;
The eye reads omens where it goes,
And speaks all languages the rose;
And, striving to be man, the worm
Mounts through all the spires of form.

II

The rounded world is fair to see,
Nine times folded in mystery:
Though baffled seers cannot impart
The secret of its laboring heart,
Throb thine with Nature's throbbing breast,
And all is clear from east to west.
Spirit that lurks each form within
Beckons to spirit of its kin;
Self-kindled every atom glows
And hints the future which it owes.

---

[1] Parts I and II originally appeared separately. Part I was published in *Nature* (1836), and Part II was published with the essay, "Nature," in *Essays* (second series, 1844).

Alphabetical List of Titles

Alphabetical List of First Lines